GW00537488

The Little Blue Book

on Retirement

By Women, For Women

Erica Baird & Karen E. Wagner

Lustre

MISSION POINT PRESS

Mission Point Press
2554 Chandler Road
Traverse City, Michigan 49696

www.MissionPointPress.com

(231) 421-9513

Printed in the United States of America

ISBN: 978-1-954786-14-1

Photography: Peter van Agtmael/Magnum Photos

Cover Illustration: Mark Pate

Introduction

When we retired, we were dismayed by how people suddenly saw us—old, done, invisible. We didn't like any of it. It wasn't how we saw ourselves, and it wasn't the way we wanted other people to see us. So we decided to fight back. We created Lustre, www.lustre.net, an online site to change the image of retired women and the picture of what retirement could be. In this book, we tell you everything we learned over the past five years. It's a quick read, but essential. We promise that if you are open to the possibilities, you will love the next third of your life.

– Karen and Erica

You will not determine my story—I will.

– Amy Schumer

Nothing in life is to be feared;

it is only to be understood.

– Marie Curie

Before You Retire.

Don't worry if you don't have a plan.

Put something on the calendar for right after you retire. Someone to meet, some place to be.

Celebrate your successful career.

Don't panic.

You will figure it out.

When one door is shut, another opens.

– *Miguel de Cervantes*

The Day You Retire.

This day will be over soon.

The only thing that ended is your job.

This is the beginning of the next third of your life.

You are the same vibrant, engaged and engaging person you were yesterday.

Champagne will help.

We really should know better than to magnify uncertainties and deficits.

– *Marianne Moore*

The First Months.
What to Do.

Sleep late. Lounge around.
Binge watch.

Find a retired friend to hang out with.

Go out. Dress up. Be seen.

Have fun. Do things you never had
time to do before.

Say "yes" to (almost) everything.

This World is not Conclusion.

A Species stands beyond–

Invisible, as Music–

But positive, as Sound–

– Emily Dickinson

Mourn.
It's Part of the Process.

You loved your career. You're sad
it's over.

The sudden loss of structure and
status is unnerving.

You don't see your people every day.
You miss them.

There's no automatic what's next.

It's scary, but you're not alone.
We all go through this.

When there are no ceilings, the sky's the limit.

– *Hillary Clinton*

Take Control. Yes, You Can.

Your time is your own. You earned the right to control it.

Try new things. Be prepared to walk away.

Do not make momentous commitments until you're sure. Go slow.

The fact that you don't have a job does not mean you're everyone's gofer. Just say no.

Relax. Breathe.

Hide not your talents,

They for use were made.

What's a sundial in the shade?

– *Benjamin Franklin*

What to Say When They Ask, "What Do You Do?"

Do not say, "I am retired" and
then stop.

Do not say, "Nothing."

Do say, "I am considering options."
If you don't have any yet, fake it.

Do talk about your passions.

Do not retreat. Stay in the mix.

That the birds of worry and care fly above your head – this you cannot change. That they build nests in your hair – this you can prevent.

– *Chinese Proverb*

Be Visible.
Style Your Retirement.

Stand tall. Shoulders back.

Radiate confidence.

Dress differently but dress.

Find your voice. You have plenty to say.

Be bold. Courage is stylish.

In olden days, a glimpse of stocking

Was looked on as something shocking.

But now, heaven knows,

Anything goes.

– *Cole Porter*

What to Wear?
Retirement Basics.

Black leather. Motorcycle jacket.

Glittery flats or sneakers.

Dress jeans.

A colorful purse–cross body and just
big enough for what you need now.

A white V-neck T.

You're always believing ahead of your evidence. What was the evidence I could write a poem? I just believed it.

– *Robert Frost*

Who Are You Now?

Your job ended. You didn't.

Your work was a big part of you.
But not all of you.

Figure out what you want to do now.

Once you do, your new identity
will emerge.

It will take time.

It is only with great difficulty, and very rarely, that I manage to be the same age every day.

– André Gide

The older I get, the greater power I seem to have to help the world. I am like a snowball, the further I am rolled, the more I gain.

– Susan B. Anthony

Own Your Age.

Be proud of your age. Tell everyone:
This is what my age looks like.

If people say you're too old for this or
that, laugh and say, "Are you serious?"

Remember your superpower:
experience.

Whatever your age, you are not old.

Remind people the only way to avoid
aging is not worth it.

If I have to, I can do anything.
I am strong, I am invincible,
I am woman.

– *Helen Reddy*

Five Fun Facts About Older and Retired Women.

There are more retired women than ever before.

Boomer women control trillions of disposable income.

Women over 50 are the wealthiest cohort in the country.

Women over 65 are likely to live until at least 90 – with their wits intact.

Boomer women will change the face of retirement.

The secret of change is to focus
all of your energy, not on fighting
the old, but on building the new.

– Socrates

Building a New Community.

Your job community is gone.
You need a new one for your new life.

Reach out to people you know.

Ask for introductions to people
you don't know.

Go places where you might meet
interesting people.

Try to meet in person when you can.
Remote is a last resort.

Stein: What is the answer?

Toklas: [Silence]

Stein: In that case, what is
the question?

– *Gertrude Stein/Alice B. Toklas*

Where Do You Want to Live?

You can live anywhere. What's it going to be?

House? Apartment? Ship? Yurt?

The familiar or the exotic?

Urban? Suburban? Beach? Woods?

Hot? Cold? Just right?

Near your family? Or far?

Leisure is a beautiful garment but it will not do for constant wear.

– *Daniel Webster*

Finding Work and Purpose.

Could you just play golf
and canasta–for decades?

If not, what do you want to
accomplish now?

Use your career and your passions
to guide you.

If you can't find just the right thing,
create it for yourself.

Trial and error is part of the journey.

For all that has been, Thanks.

To all that shall be, Yes.

– Dag Hammarskjöld

Retirement Surprises. Eventually.

Time is your new asset.

You've moved on. You actually don't want your old job back.

Your career is foundational in unexpected ways.

Retirement can be cool.

Retirement can empower the rebel in you.

About the Authors

After they retired, Erica and Karen founded Lustre, www.lustre.net, to challenge stereotypes about retirement and older women and create a new framework for what modern retirement can look like for modern women. They are both lawyers who loved practicing law for over four decades. They were both firsts: Karen was the first female litigation partner in her global law firm, and Erica was the first female partner in the General Counsel's Office of a then Big 8 accounting firm. Erica and Karen both live in Manhattan.

Notes

Notes

Printed in the USA
CPSIA information can be obtained
at www.ICGtesting.com
LVHW051541150424
777458LV00010B/211

9 781954 786226